So Nick can look at
reptiles better when he is
seven.

Happy Birthday —
Mom — dad
July 11, 1975

Let's Look at Reptiles

Some other books by Harriet E. Huntington

Let's Go Outdoors
Let's Go to the Brook
Let's Go to the Desert
Let's Go to the Seashore
Let's Go to the Woods
Let's Look at Flowers
Let's Look at Insects

Let's Look at Reptiles

Written and illustrated with photographs
by Harriet E. Huntington

Drawings by J. Noël

Doubleday & Company, Garden City, New York

ISBN: 0-385-08273-8 TRADE
ISBN: 0-385-04853-X PREBOUND
Library of Congress Catalog Card Number 73-76447
Copyright © 1973 by Harriet E. Huntington
All Rights Reserved
Printed in the United States of America
9   8   7   6   5   4   3   2

Dedicated
to
Joseph Faddler
in gratitude for the help he has
given me with the photography
in this and other books.

Contents

Let's Look at Reptiles

Introduction

Let's look at reptiles. A reptile is a cold-blooded animal which has scales, a backbone, lays eggs on land or gives birth to live young, and breathes air. Crocodiles, alligators, lizards, snakes, and turtles are reptiles. This book is about reptiles in the United States. You can find them in backyards, parks, meadows, woods, forests, in or near streams, ponds, lakes, deserts, and upon mountains. They crawl on the ground, dig down into the soil, climb trees, and swim. Some reptiles, such as the alligator, grow to be almost twelve feet long, while others, like the Florida reef gecko lizard, are only two and a half inches long. Some reptiles, such as sea turtles, may weigh as much as five hundred pounds, yet others, like the blind snake, are about as heavy as a fat fishing worm.

The main differences between reptiles and other animals is that all reptiles have scales or horny plates on their bodies. A salamander may look very much like a lizard but it does not have scales. However, animals which have scales are not always reptiles. For instance, fish are covered with scales and birds have scales on their legs and feet.

About 300 million years ago, when the earth was covered with shallow seas, swamps, and forests of seed ferns and other tropical primitive plants, the first reptiles began to live on land. Paleontologists, men who study fossils or the remains of ancient animals, believe that reptiles evolved from amphibians. Amphibians—salamanders, frogs, and toads—live both in water and on land, but they must go back to the water to lay their eggs. Because if these eggs, which are enveloped in a mass of jelly, were laid on land they would soon dry up and the embryo or undeveloped baby amphibian would die. However, the reptiles developed an egg that had a rubbery coating, or shell, which protected the egg. As millions of years passed, some reptiles developed into dinosaurs and birds—most of which no longer exist. Today, there are a few descendants, such as the crocodiles, alligators, turtles, lizards, birds, and mammals. If you are ever asked the question, "Which came first, the chicken or the egg?" you can say "the egg" because the reptile ancestors of birds laid eggs which eventually evolved into chickens.

The reptile egg was a big development in the process of evolution. Reptiles could wander all over the land and were not forced to return to water to lay their eggs as the amphibians do. The reptile embryo was able to develop a miniature adult body before it hatched and did not have to go through the polliwog stage of growing legs and losing a tail. The reptile egg had a yolk which contained chemicals, such as fats, sugars, starches, and proteins. In the reptile egg, the yolk is attached to the embryo by an umbilical cord. The skinlike wall or membrane of the yolk has veins which carry blood filled with nutritious chemicals into the embryo. The embryo is enclosed in a sac called the amnion. This sac is filled with a liquid which cushions and protects the growing embryo. Inside the egg there is a third sac, called the allantois, into which waste products accumulate. Most reptile shells have microscopic pores which let oxygen in and carbon dioxide out. The membranous lining of the shell, called the chorion, has veins with blood cells which absorb oxygen. The chorion is connected to the membranous wall of the amniotic sac. The carbon dioxide from the amniotic sac is absorbed by blood cells and carried to the chorion where it is released through the shell pores. Usually the contents of the yolk sac is used before the reptile hatches, but sometimes the empty sac breaks off after the young one is a few days old. Some reptiles, like the turtles, carry their sacs for several weeks.

Many lizards and snakes lay eggs, but a few give birth to their young. These are called viviparous. Some snakes, like the copperhead, are born enclosed in a transparent membrane sac. Others, like the red-bellied snake, are born alive.

Reptiles, such as turtles, crocodiles, and alligators, hatch from eggs which have been laid in nests. To open their shells, the baby snakes and lizards have an egg tooth which is attached to the tip of their snouts. The egg tooth is somewhat like their other teeth but is bigger, curves forward, and is razor-sharp. Usually this egg tooth falls off the day the reptile hatches, but it may remain a day or so longer. Crocodiles, alligators, and turtles do not have a true egg tooth. Instead they have a horny scalelike structure, called the egg caruncle, which is set at the tip of their snout or beak and also is shed after hatching.

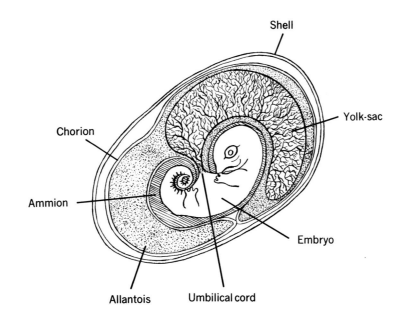

Lizards

Lizards, like all reptiles, are vertebrates. A vertebrate is an animal which has a backbone made up of small bones called vertebrae. Vertebrates have a skull to protect their brains and ribs to protect their lungs, heart, stomach, and other organs. In the center of their backbone is the spinal nerve cord which connects the nerves of the animal to its brain. Some reptiles, like lizards, have extra-long backbones or tails.

On the opposite page the drawing on the left shows a skeleton of a collared lizard. In this drawing you can see the skull, backbone, ribs, and the various bones of its legs and feet. The back legs are attached to a hipbone or pelvic girdle, while the shortened front legs are connected to a shoulder bone or pectoral girdle.

In the drawing on the right you can see where the six main parts of the digestive system —mouth, esophagus or throat, stomach, small intestine, large intestine, and a cloaca are found inside the body. The cloaca, which is a cavity between the intestines and anal opening, receives the waste products of digestion.

Most lizards do not store urine in a bladder, or excrete water in their urine, but conserve their body fluids. Their urine is pastelike and their bladder is quite small. This enables some of the lizards to live on the hot, dry deserts. The outside opening to the cloaca is a slit in the skin. This opening, called the vent, is on the underside of the belly at the base of the tail.

Female lizards lay their eggs in sand, loose soil, among leaves, under logs or rocks, where they will be protected from rainy and cold weather. Lizards do not sit on their eggs as birds do to keep them warm so that they will hatch. Usually lizard eggs are laid in the early summer and hatch two or three months later. Depending upon the species, the female lays from one to twenty eggs.

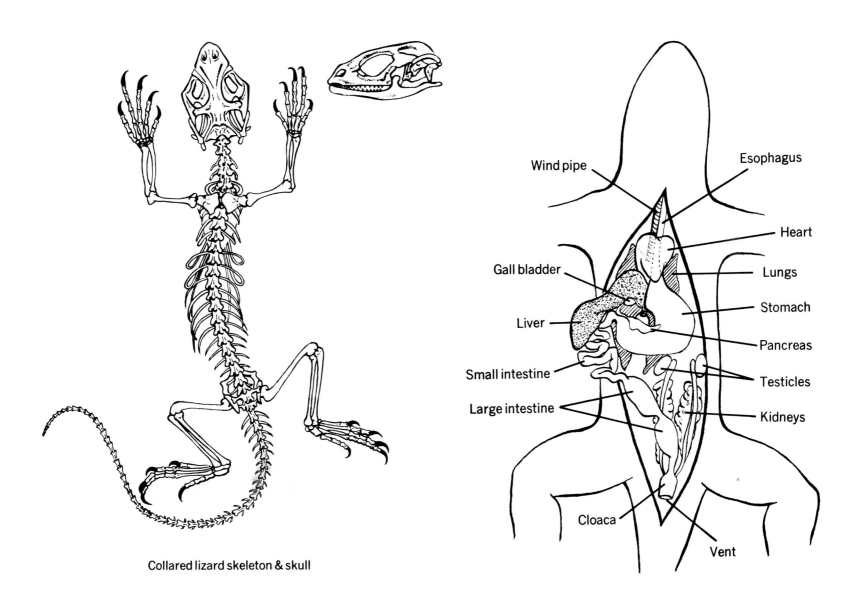

Wind pipe

Esophagus

Heart

Gall bladder

Lungs

Liver

Stomach

Pancreas

Small intestine

Testicles

Large intestine

Kidneys

Cloaca

Vent

Collared lizard skeleton & skull

All reptiles are cold-blooded or ectothermal—"ecto" means outside and "thermal" means heat. Reptiles do not have the kind of body which creates its own heat and keeps the blood at a steady temperature. Their blood absorbs heat and becomes about the same temperature as that of the surrounding air, ground, or rocks. When reptiles are in the shade, their blood is colder than if they were in direct sunlight, absorbing the heat from the sun. On a cold day you will see lizards sunning themselves on warm rocks. They emerge in the morning, disappear at noon when the sun is at its hottest, and reappear in the late afternoon. However, some lizards do have the ability to control, within a few degrees of temperature, the amount of heat that their bodies can absorb. When their bodies are cold, their skin is darkish and it absorbs heat. As they warm up, their skin becomes lighter and it reflects heat. To change from dark to light, the particles of color in their skin contract and let in light. To change from light to dark, the particles of color expand to shut out light.

Lizards will not eat until they are warm enough to move quickly and catch their prey. When lizards have eaten a lot of food and have stored up energy, they do not become hungry until they have used up the stored energy and need more. After the desert iguanas have had their morning sunshine and are warmed up, they scamper across the sand to climb up the branches of the creosote bushes and other plants to reach and eat the tender leaves, buds, and flowers. Occasionally they eat insects. But this is not unusual because many lizards are carnivorous. If you are collecting lizards in the countryside, be careful which ones you put together or you may have one or two fewer by the time you arrive home. Some lizards are cannibalistic and eat other lizards.

Desert Iguana

The desert spiny lizard is so named because it lives in deserts and because it has pointed or spinelike scales. These lizards have colorful scales and can readily be seen when they are sunning on rocks. However, they are not easy to catch because they are extremely alert and ready to run at the slightest threat of danger. When lizards run quickly, they use their claws to grasp hold of the dirt or sand and pull-push themselves forward. Often lizards sunbathe near some little animal's abandoned burrow, in which they can hide if threatened, especially by predatory birds.

The desert spiny lizards are able to withstand colder temperatures than some other lizards and have been found high up in the mountains. They hibernate during the winter months in crevices of granite boulders. To hibernate is to go into a kind of resting period during which time their heartbeat and breathing is so slow that it almost appears that all body functions have stopped. The older lizards go farther into the rock crevices and remain until spring while the younger or first-year ones stay closer to the crevice openings so that they can get out to hunt during the occasional hot, short autumn days. Depending upon the species and climate, lizards hibernate in sand, among leaves, under rocks, and down into the ground below the freezing line, maybe from three inches to three feet.

Desert Spiny Lizard

The chuckwalla is one of the largest lizards in the United States. Some adult ones measure one and one-half feet from the tip of their snouts to the tip of their tails. In the photograph you can see a young chuckwalla at the farther end of the rock. This lizard is colored olive with darker stripes while its tail has black and olive-yellow bands. The hands, legs, and undersides of most adult chuckwallas are colored darkish brown with white spots. As lizards grow older their color patterns change. Crossbands become fainter, stripes disappear, and many adults are mottled. Their skin, covered with tiny granular or rounded scales, is loose around the neck and at the sides it hangs in wrinkles and folds over their stubby, flat bodies.

In the photograph you can see the ear, which looks like a round hole about the size of a pea and is behind the eye and before the neck fold. The eardrum is a transparent thin disk made of skinlike tissue which is somewhat like wax paper. The eardrum is protected by a group of enlarged pointed scales. Lizards use their hearing to warn them of approaching dangers or to locate insects burrowing in the sand. If they hear a sound that may sound like an insect moving, they will cock their head to one side in order to hear better. Most lizards have ears but no voice. Only the gecko lizards make a chirping sound. Herpetologists, scientists who study reptiles, say these lizards may use the chirp to attract a mate or to frighten enemies.

Chuckwalla

Coyotes, foxes, hawks, and owls eat desert lizards like the chuckwalla. When a chuckwalla is frightened, it takes refuge in a rock crevice. Then, to protect itself from being pulled out, it will gulp air into its lungs and inflate its body until it is firmly wedged in between the rocks, and practically no amount of tugging can remove it. Sometimes, chuckwallas will hold their breath for a long time. Because chuckwallas, like most lizards, do not need a large amount of oxygen, they do not have to breathe so often. Only when the lizard feels safe will it let out the air and cautiously venture forth.

Some lizards have binocular vision, similar to yours. This means the field of vision of the two eyes overlap, enabling the lizard to judge distances and perceive depths. Therefore they can pounce upon their prey with accuracy. Inside their eyes, lizards have yellow oil droplets which act like sunglasses and filter out excess light. Some lizards have a third eye, called the pineal eye, which is located on the top of their head behind their two eyes. This eye is very small and looks like a tiny whitish scale. It is a light-sensing organ and can tell if a shadow crosses over it, thus warning the lizard of a possible attack from above. Scientists believe that the pineal eye helps the lizard to tell how much sunlight or heat its body is receiving.

Chuckwalla in a Rock Crevice

Alligator lizards are so named because their short bodies, stubby legs, and long tails make them look a little bit like miniature alligators. However, their brownish scales are not tough or horny like those of an alligator but are spiny and flat. These lizards have a very long tail, almost twice as long as the body. Different kinds of alligator lizards are found throughout the western United States and Mexico. They live in grasslands, oak-studded rolling hills, forests, and canyon bottoms, where there are lots of plants which they can climb in search of prey. Those which live near streams will sometimes go into the water to escape from enemies. Most lizards can swim if it is necessary, and when they do, they wriggle their tails like fish and alligators.

Lizards use their tongues to both smell and taste. As they prowl in search of food, they test things to find out about them by tasting them with their tongues. When the lizards smell with their tongues, they slowly lick the air and then withdraw the tongues coated with the microscopic particles of airborne odors. The tongue puts these particles into the opening of a sense organ called Jacobson's organ. This opening is in the roof of the mouth rather than in the nasal passage as it is in mammals. Lizards can follow the fresh trail of their prey by using their tongues and their Jacobson's organs.

Alligator Lizard

The body of a lizard is protected by scales. A scale is made up of a horny substance, something like your fingernail. Scales are various sizes and shapes in different parts of the lizard body. Each species has its particular pattern which makes them easy to identify. Usually a few of the scales on the head are larger than those on the body. These scales are named according to their location, such as postocular, meaning behind the eyes. On spiny lizards most scales are of a diamond shape and they overlap like shingles on a roof. The scales on the back and sides have ridges or keels which end in sharply pointed spines. Other lizards have scales which are embedded in the skin and are square-, oblong-, triangular- or round-shaped.

Scales grow in and are part of the skin. The inner layer, called the dermis, is thick and has color particles, nerves, and a few blood cells; the outer layer, called the epidermis, is thin, and the scales are embedded in it. In between the overlapping scales is a fold of skin, called the hinge, which stretches. This is convenient not only when lizards inflate themselves but when they move in any way, whether they stretch an arm, a leg, or turn their head.

Granite Spiny Lizard

As a lizard grows larger, its scales grow bigger and the outside skinlike covering becomes too small. Then the lizard molts or sheds its old skin. Lizards which have a rough skin or sharp spiny scales, such as the granite spiny or fence lizards, tend to shed their skin in large flakes, somewhat the way your skin would peel after a bad sunburn. Some lizards, like the alligator or legless lizards, tend to shed their skin in one piece. The skin begins to peel around the lips and folds back as the lizard wriggles and crawls out of it. Before it dried and became somewhat stiff, the lizard skin in the photograph was like a soft, pliable, paper-thin piece of plastic.

To remove its skin the lizard may rub against rocks and tree trunks. This takes some lizards a day or two, while others need more time, often several weeks. If the skin sticks, the lizard will loosen and soften it by soaking in a mud puddle or nearby stream. If you ever watch a gecko shed and see it pull the skin off its front legs with its mouth, you might think it looks as though it were taking off a glove. Almost all lizards shed upon coming out of hibernation. Some species shed every two or three weeks, while others shed only once or twice a year. Geckos and some other lizards eat their old skin as it is shed.

Alligator Lizard Skin

Fence lizards, as you might guess by their name, are often found on fences but they are also seen on logs, piles of lumber, sides of buildings, and rocks. Fence lizards are also called "swifts" and "blue bellies." If you have ever tried to catch a swift, you will know that they are well named because they can run extremely fast. There are about thirty different kinds of swifts in the United States and they all look and behave somewhat the same. The spiny scales on their backs and legs are colored gray, tan, brown, or black, while the undersides of the bellies are blue. Some male swifts have a few scattered blue or green scales on their backs but the females are pale and drab.

Many lizards, like the alligator and fence lizards, have a way of defending themselves by losing their tails. If a lizard is caught by its tail, it can quickly twist itself and break off the tail. Sometimes when it is running away from an enemy, the lizard will drop off its tail. The discarded tail will wiggle and twitch after it has been dropped. This can distract the enemy and make him forget to continue chasing the lizard. If the collared and leopard lizards lose their tails, they cannot grow another but some other lizards can. The new tail is never as long as the old one and does not have vertebrae. Instead, in its center is a kind of rod made up of a horny substance like gristle which is covered with flesh and skin. The scales, colors, and patterns are slightly different from the old tail. Occasionally, if a hind leg is bitten off, a tail-like stump will grow. This stump may help to balance the lizard. However, the stump does not develop feet.

Western Fence Lizard

The horned lizard, or toad, has two or more large sharp spines on its head. Smaller pointed scales fringe the sides of its body and tail, while its back is spotted with large pointed scales. Horned lizards are not easy to find—not only because their scales are patterned so as to camouflage them against the sand or soil, but also because their body is flat and casts no shadow to betray its presence. When alerted they will sometimes stay very still so that they will blend in with the ground and not be noticed. If they are frightened, they may squirt blood from the corner of their eyes to scare away the enemy. Sometimes they will inflate their body by gulping in air, which makes the spines on their back stand up so that the lizard seems to increase in size and thereby frighten its enemy. Being inflated makes them hard to swallow by snakes. The spines can pierce the mouth, throat, and stomach of the enemy.

These lizards bury themselves in the sand to escape being noticed by predators, as well as to escape from the heat of the sun at noontime. They also dig themselves into the sand when they go to sleep at night. To bury itself, the lizard uses its wedged-shaped head as a bulldozer and pushes itself with its front legs until it is half-hidden. Then, with its back legs, it moves in a kind of wiggly dance until all but its tail is under, then the tail swishes from side to side and disappears. These lizards are most often found on the ground where they can reach ants. Horned lizards need to have three or four varieties of ants to remain healthy, and they may eat as many as 300 to 400 a day.

Horned Lizard

Alligator Lizards

Collared Lizard

Most lizards do not chew or grind with their teeth. Instead, they use them to catch and hold onto their prey or to bite off a leaf or bud and to puncture the flesh of their victim so that the digestive juices can immediately begin to work. The teeth of lizards in the United States do not grow in sockets, like yours, but are attached to the inner surface of the jawbones. If lizards lose one of these teeth, another will grow in its place. Some lizards, like the iguanas, have two different shapes of teeth. Those at the front of the jaws are sharp and conelike, while those in rows at the sides of the jaws are flat and triangular.

Sometimes when a lizard sees an insect it will twitch its tail, like a cat, before it pounces. It lunges with open jaws and snaps them around the prey, shaking it several times in order to stun it so that it will not struggle. Then the lizard maneuvers the insect around so that its head goes first down the throat and its legs will fold back against its belly. If the legs stuck out, the lizard would have trouble swallowing it. The lizard swallows its prey all in one piece. Sometimes if the animal is large, the lizard has to struggle to get it down. Then, after the lizard is able to close its mouth, it bends its head back and forth to force the insect down the throat and into the stomach. After the animal has completely disappeared, the lizard often remains in one spot while it digests the food.

Alligator Lizard Eating a Cricket

Gila Monster

The only poisonous lizard in the United States is the Gila monster. Gila, prounced "hela," is the Spanish name of the river in Arizona where these lizards were first discovered. This is the largest lizard in North America. Some Gila monsters, when full grown, weigh four pounds and are two feet long. The Gila monster can be found from the southeastern border of Arizona up into Utah and Nevada and just across the Colorado River into California. It roams on the lower slopes of the desert mountains and canyon bottoms where there are streams. The scales on its back are beadlike, while those on its belly are squarish. The orange-yellow or pink and brown or black markings act as camouflage in the dim light of dusk or dawn during the summer. The black blends into the shadows, while the orange-yellow resembles pebbles or sticks.

This lizard hunts bird and reptile eggs, baby birds, and small animals, but very seldom does it eat adult lizards. It uses its poison or venom to paralyze its prey. The venom is in a concentrated solution of saliva which, when injected into the victim, begins the digestive process. The poisonous saliva glands are in the lower jaw—not like rattlesnakes, which have their fangs and poison glands in their upper jaw. These glands are not connected to the teeth as they are in rattlesnakes but discharge their poison through a duct or tube which is at the base of the teeth and lip. The lizard grips and chews, puncturing many holes into which the poison enters the victim.

Like most animals, the Gila monster is not dangerous unless disturbed, molested, or teased. However, to protect itself, it may lash out or strike out very quickly with its mouth open and if you happen to be close enough it might bite you. Very seldom is the bite fatal to a human, but it causes a severe local pain and swelling and creates a weakness that may last for several days.

Because the lizard in the photograph has two black rings bordered with narrow white ones around its neck, it is called a collared lizard. These lizards are most brilliantly colored. Not all collared lizards are so colorful. They may be a dull gray or brown, with mottled patterns of white and black. Female collared lizards have about the same markings, but the colors look drab. As lizards grow old their colors have a tendency to fade.

Most male animals defend certain areas over which they claim a kind of ownership. Usually these areas are their hunting grounds or nesting places and trespassers are fought off. Consequently a male with a brilliant display of colors would discourage another male from intruding on his territory. Sometimes you will see a male bobbing up and down as though he were doing pushups. This is a gesture of warning to intruders to stay away. If the trespasser bobs back, it is a male, if it does not, it is a female. Lizards cannot always tell whether another lizard is a male or female except by its behavior.

Collared lizards are found in desert regions west of the Mississippi. They live in canyons, gullies, and on mountain slopes, where there are rocks and open spaces for running. They are usually found up on a rock rather than down on the ground so that they can see their prey more easily. If you ever watched a collared lizard run, using only its strong hind legs, while holding up its short front legs close to its chest and with its tail raised, you might think that it looked like a miniature dinosaur. Collared lizards are aggressive and pugnacious creatures and do not make good pets because they bite. As one might suspect by their behavior, they are carnivorous and eat many lizards, snakes, and rodents, as well as large insects, such as grasshoppers.

Collared Lizard

As its name implies, the granite night lizard lives among granite rocks and roams about at night. These lizards are grayish tan, with large dark brown spots. When they are under granite flakes they are dark—their spots are large while the tan lines between them are narrow. But when the lizards are exposed to sunlight these tan lines become wider, making the spots look smaller. Thus the lizard camouflages itself and blends with the granite. If they are very excited they tend to become lighter. The colors change quickly or slowly depending upon the temperature or humidity, whether it is night or day, or the emotions of the lizard.

Lizards that sleep at night and stay awake during the day have eyes with rounded pupils, like yours, while lizards that sleep during the day and hunt at night have slit pupils, like a cat. If you look at the lizard on the opposite page, you can tell by its eyes that it is active at night. These lizards have no movable eyelids, so they cannot blink. Instead, to wipe off a bit of dust or dirt, the lizard flips out its tongue, moves it over its eye, and the speck is gone. These lizards have a transparent scale which covers and protects the eye.

Granite night lizards are rather small, measuring about five or six inches from snout to tail tip. During the daytime, granite night lizards almost always stay hidden under thin pieces of granite rock, but at night they come out to look for prey. Sometimes they sit on the rock waiting for moths and other insects to come close enough to be caught. At other times they go hunting for insects, spiders, ticks, scorpions, and centipedes. Once in a while, like other carnivorous lizards, they need to have vegetables in their diet, so they eat a few plant leaves.

Granite Night Lizard

The two lizards among the leaves in the photograph are anoles. Although these lizards may change their colors from green to brown and are often mistakenly called chameleons, they are not true chameleons. True chameleons are found in Africa, southern India, and Madagascar. Anoles are found in the southeastern part of the United States, but you can find them also in some pet stores. Unlike true chameleons, anoles do not change their color to match whatever color they happen to be upon. Anoles do not change the white of their bellies or chins. When they turn green or brown, it is because their skin reacts to heat or cold and to darkness or light. When they are in the forest, the light which filters through the leaves above them causes their skin to turn green, even though they may be sitting on a brown branch.

The males have a hanging fold of skin, called a dewlap, under their chin. Inside the dewlap is a bony rod which is attached to the jaw. When the male lizard bobs his head as a gesture of defense of his territory, the rod moves out and stretches the dewlap, making it look like a large double chin. As the dewlap is extended, the bright red skin between the white scales is exposed and this display of unexpected color frightens the intruder away.

Anoles live among bushes, trees, fences, and old wooden buildings. They jump from branch to branch in order to catch insects. As is true with many lizards in captivity, anoles do not drink water from a dish. If you have one for a pet, offer it leaves sprinkled with drops of water, like dew. Then watch it lap up the drops with its little tongue.

Anoles

The life-size animal in the photograph looks very much like a small snake, but it is a leg-less lizard. You can see in the insert picture that its eyes are small and have lids, which the lizard closes when it burrows. Its shovel-shaped snout helps it to burrow under the soil. Its lower jaw fits into the upper one so that grains of sand and dirt will not get into its mouth. When it travels underground, it moves its body from side to side like a snake and is often found about two or three inches below the surface. Because its shiny, rounded, and over-lapping scales are slippery and smooth, they allow the lizard to move easily through loose soil. Its tiny forked tongue can be protruded through a slit at the tip of its snout so that when it wants to smell, it does not have to open its jaws. This can be convenient when underground and tracking an insect prey. Usually it forages under the soil for insect larvae. Occasionally, it comes out at night to hunt for small spiders and insects.

These lizards live in sandy washes, loamy soil, and in sand along the coast of California. Because their skin has a tendency to dry out, they need to be where they can find moist earth. During the daytime these lizards may stay under rocks and logs, or dig down beneath clumps of plants, even trees. Those which live at the beaches hide under driftwood or plants. The lizard in the photograph is gray or tan on its back, with black lines and a pale yellow on its undersides. Other legless lizards may be dark brown with a yellow belly.

California Legless Lizard

Crocodiles and Alligators

Crocodiles and alligators belong to the same family and look somewhat alike. One quick way to tell them apart is by the shape of their heads. Crocodiles have a triangular head with a long narrow snout, while alligators have a broad head with a short blunt snout. The nostrils and eyes are on top of the head, and by keeping these parts out of water they can see and breathe when they swim, float, or rest at the edge of a river, lake, pond, or swamp hollow.

The inside body structure of these animals is somewhat different from other reptiles. The heart has four chambers or compartments. A four-chambered heart is better able to send blood all over the body. Because crocodiles and alligators do not have lips which can be shut to make their mouths airtight, they have, at the back of the tongue, a large flap or fold of skin which can be moved upward so as to close off the mouth from the air passage to the lungs. This is important because when these animals are under water and the flap is closed, water cannot enter their lungs. They do not use their teeth to chew, but to hold onto and bite or tear off pieces of their prey. The peglike teeth, like those of dinosaurs, are set in sockets which are around the edges of the jawbones. The stomach is divided into two sections. One section, which is called the gizzard, is the larger and has thick muscular walls which contract and expand to mix up the food. In the gizzard are pebbles which the animal periodically swallows and which act like teeth grinding the food into small pieces. Behind the gizzard is a smaller section which opens into the intestines.

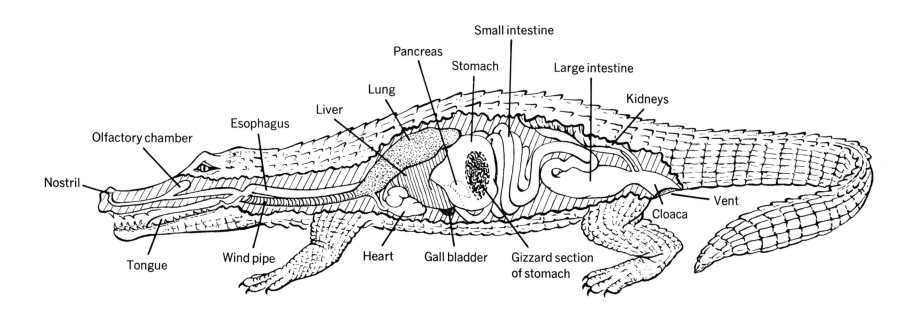

Small intestine

Pancreas

Stomach

Large intestine

Lung

Liver

Kidneys

Esophagus

Olfactory chamber

Nostril

Vent

Cloaca

Tongue

Wind pipe

Heart

Gall bladder

Gizzard section
of stomach

Alligators live near fresh water in the tropical climate of southeastern United States, while the North American crocodiles are found in the salt marshes of southern Florida. Because they are cold-blooded animals they either cool themselves off in water or warm themselves on land in the sunshine. Alligators have several ways of land travel. They can crawl slowly on their bellies with their legs sprawled out, or they can go quickly and almost slide over the ground, particularly when they are gliding down a riverbank into the water. On land the alligator usually is slow and seemingly clumsy as it carries its heavy body up off the ground and balances it on short stubby legs. The animal alternately puts down both left feet and then both right feet, swinging its hip and shoulder forward with each step. When it decides upon a place for sunbathing, it stops walking, lowers its body and head onto the ground, and then spreads out its front and hind legs to the side. Completely relaxed, it looks as though it had collapsed from the exertion.

An alligator has five toes on its front feet and its hind feet have only four. The hind feet are webbed to help it swim while the front feet have separate toes and claws for digging. These the alligator needs when it makes a den for winter hibernation. It digs down into the banks of streams or lakes to make a cavelike room large enough for it to turn around in. The entrance is usually under water but the den above the waterline is filled with air.

The alligator uses its tail like a fish for swimming and glides gracefully through water, while its legs and feet are held streamlined against its body. Its tail is also a weapon of defense which the alligator can lash back and forth in a battle with an enemy. Alligators hiss when disturbed and will hold their mouths open as a defense gesture.

Alligator

Because an alligator can maneuver better in the water, it often lies in wait for prey to come close enough to the water's edge so that it can lunge with open jaws and grab the animal. If the prey is too large to gulp down in one mouthful, it is shaken violently, torn into pieces, and then swallowed.

During the early spring nights, one can hear the alligator males roaring to the females in a series of short but loud bellows. Later in the spring, after she has mated, the female alligator builds a nest for her eggs. She scoops up grasses, branches, and mud with her lower jaw to make a mound. She lays between twenty and seventy eggs in the center and then covers them with more mud and plants until the mound is about three feet high and from four to seven feet wide. As the plants decompose they give off a constant heat which allows the eggs to develop and hatch.

For the next two and a half months, until the eggs hatch, she stays around guarding the nest because if she did not, her eggs could be found and eaten by raccoons, skunks, bears, and wild hogs. When the eggs hatch and she hears the babies grunting, she tears the nest apart so that the eight- or nine-inch-long baby alligators can get out. The babies hunt for shrimp, water insects, and crabs, but as they grow bigger they eat snakes, lizards, toads, turtles, and fish. By the time they are adults they are eating mammals and water birds.

Alligator in Water

Crocodiles and alligators have three eyelids. The lower lid is larger than the upper lid and both of them close when the animal goes to sleep. The third lid under the other two goes across the eye from front to back. This lid keeps the eye clean by pushing bits of dirt and dust into the corner of the eye where they later can fall off. You might say an alligator blinks with its third eyelid.

The crocodile and alligator have ears which are behind the eyes and are covered with a flap of skin. In front of the flap is a slit through which airborne sounds enter. This slit closes when the creature submerges. When crocodiles dive, or go under water, they shut the opening to their external nostrils. To do this there is a muscle, just below the skin, which pushes against the wall of the nasal passage to close it off, and when the muscle pulls back, it opens the nostril.

On the back of the crocodile and alligator are rows of dark brown, ridged, horny plates, while on their legs, tail, and undersides are tough leathery scales. As the animal grows so do the plates and scales, but, instead of molting, the old outer skin of the scales rubs or wears off. As it ages, its skin becomes a dull gray.

Crocodiles and alligators kept in zoos live to be about fifty years old. We do not know how old they may become when they are in the wild, but presumably they do not live as long because in zoos they are protected and are fed regularly. The average length of adult alligators is between six and twelve feet and North American crocodiles between seven and twelve feet. However, some alligators have grown to be about nineteen feet long and crocodiles to about fifteen feet long.

Crocodile on Log

Turtles

The inside organs of the turtle are about the same as those of the lizard, but the skeleton is very different. The top of a turtle shell is called a carapace and the bottom is called the plastron. These parts which protect the internal organs are connected at the sides. If you look at the drawing of the underside of the carapace, you can see where the backbone runs down the center of the shell and how the ribs have branched off to develop into the shell. The neck and tail are continuations of the backbone. The inside of the shell is made of bone, but the outside is covered with horny scales. Both shell and scales grow as the turtle becomes larger. However, the turtle does not molt as do lizards. Instead, the scales on the shell flake off or peel as new and larger scales are formed under the old ones. Sometimes the old scales are just worn away.

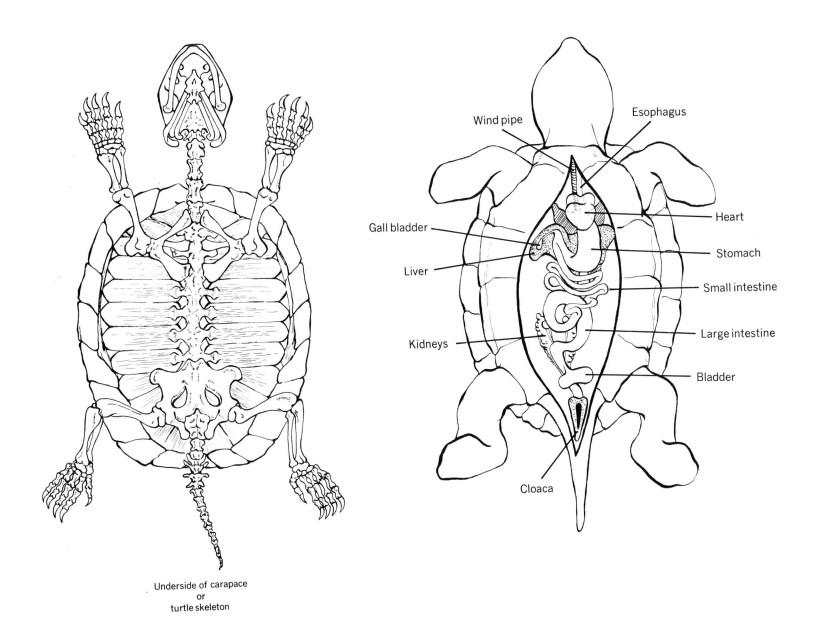

Wind pipe

Esophagus

Gall bladder

Liver

Kidneys

Heart

Stomach

Small intestine

Large intestine

Bladder

Cloaca

Underside of carapace
or
turtle skeleton

When the animal withdraws its head, legs, and tail into the shell, its body is protected. While the shell gives a tortoise protection, it also restricts its movements. The animal cannot bend forward, backward, or to the side, and it has to turn all the way around to see what is behind it. The shell is awkward, and often when climbing, the tortoise has to slither and slide over rocks, landing with a bump. The hind legs of a desert tortoise look a little like those of an elephant except that the tortoise has legs which are covered with scales. Most turtles have five short claws on each foot, but there are two exceptions in American turtles. The desert tortoise has five toes on its front feet and four toes on its hind feet, while the box turtle has three toes on each hind foot.

The Latin name for these desert tortoises is *Gopherus* because they tunnel like gophers. These tunnels which are dug in firm ground, such as banks of desert washes, are from three to thirty feet long and may hold from one to ten or more tortoises. The short tunnels are dug for temporary shelter, while the long ones, called dens, are occupied when the tortoises hibernate or estivate. To estivate is to spend the hot dry summer in a kind of resting period like hibernation.

The desert tortoise males are extremely belligerent toward other males and attack without provocation. They use the pointed projection at the front of their shell to overturn the opponent. You can see this projection just below the head of the male on the right in the photograph. Tortoises fight until one withdraws or is turned over onto its back. Then the loser must turn himself back onto his feet or die. If he is in the desert sunlight, the heat will cook him to death in an hour or two. Before they fight, the male guarding his territory will bob his head as a gesture of defense.

Desert Tortoises

Box turtles, like the ones in the photograph, have plastrons which are divided into three sections or flaps. The front and back flaps are hinged to the center section and can fold upward to fit into and against the carapace. When the head, legs, and tail are withdrawn and these flaps are closed, the little creature is protected against foxes, skunks, or pigs, which are unable to open its shell. In fact, the muscle which holds them together is so strong that a man cannot open them with his bare hands. Turtles which live on land, and a few which live both on land and in water, have thick skin on their heads and necks but large scales on the exposed side of their legs and feet. You can see in the drawing how the turtle bends its neck into an S-curve when it withdraws its head. When turtles hibernate they withdraw themselves into their shell.

Turtles do not hear as well as alligators or lizards. The box turtle can hear low and deep sounds which are just audible to a human. The wood turtle can hear a little better a few tones higher. Turtles do not depend upon their hearing as much as other reptiles do. Turtle ears are similar to those of lizards and their eardrums are covered by skin.

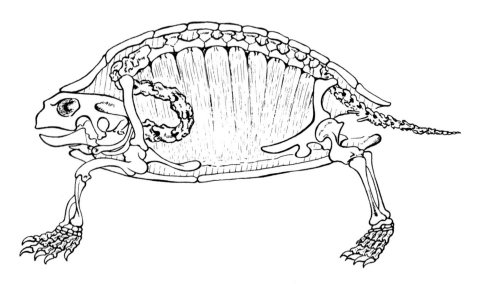

Side view of how turtle bends neck to pull back its head into shell

Western Box Turtle

Box turtles make good pets and often a group of owners will gather together to have a turtle race. A circle with a diameter from ten to sixteen feet is drawn, and in its center are placed four or five turtles. They are put into a corral or enclosure, which is usually a cardboard box with its top and bottom cut away. When the race begins, the corral is lifted and whichever turtle reaches the edge of the circle first—wins. The turtle on the preceding page is a champion and has won many races for its owner. Some turtle clubs even have steeplechases with miniature hills, ponds, and other hazards.

Box Turtle

Some turtles have scales with ridges or rings like the wood turtle in the photograph. You cannot count these ridges and tell how many years the turtle has lived because the ridges are growth marks and two or three may be formed in a year. Sometimes there is more food than at other times and the turtles grow faster. While it is difficult to tell exactly how old a tortoise may be, they do live to be as old, if not older, than humans.

Wood turtles make better pets than most other turtles because they are more intelligent, have an even temper, and rarely ever bite. They also are healthier and are less sensitive to temperature changes and therefore less prone to having colds. Some wood turtles have been tested and found to have an intelligence equal to that of a rat. Some pet turtles have been known to "beg" for food. One in particular, when it came out of hibernation and was hungry, would scratch on the screen door, wait to be let into the house, and then go the shortest route to the refrigerator. Needless to say the owner had fed it from the refrigerator before and the turtle remembered.

Wood Turtle

Soft-shelled turtles have a bony shell which is covered with a leathery skin. These turtles dig down into the mud or sand on the bottom of ponds, canals, or quiet streams. They conceal themselves with only their heads protruding and wait for a shrimp, frog, or fish. When one comes close enough, the turtle stretches its long neck and grabs it. Their jaws are covered with loose skin and when they burrow the skin keeps grains of sand out of their mouths. When they dig they use their heads to start burrowing and their front flippers to throw sand over their backs until they are covered. Then the turtles stick their long snorklelike snouts out. Their color is drab olive gray which blends with sand and the muddy bottom.

Turtles, because they are cold-blooded, do not need a lot of oxygen and therefore do not breathe often. Sometimes one deep breath may be enough to last for two hours. Turtles, like the soft-shell turtle, have a way of "breathing" while under water. To do this the turtle sucks water into its throat, does not swallow, and then expels it. The turtle can absorb the oxygen in the water through the walls of its pharynx which is the area at the back of its throat. Some turtles also absorb oxygen through two thin-walled sacs connected to the cloaca. These sacs are filled with water and emptied by the turtle opening the cloaca. In other words both the pharynx and the cloaca sacs act as gills. The pair of lungs are flattish and are placed close together against the carapace just behind the pectoral girdle.

Soft-shelled Turtle

The alligator snapping turtle has a very small plastron. Being carnivorous, aggressive, and agile, it does not need as much protection as the slow-moving box turtle. Like an alligator, this turtle has brown, spiked scales upon its back and tail. When it is resting on the river or canal bottom, it can scarcely be seen because it looks so much like its surroundings. Because its beak is sharp and its jaws have powerful muscles, the turtle can inflict a savage wound. This turtle grows to be very large. In fact, it is the largest fresh-water turtle in North America. Its carapace may measure more than two feet and its body may weigh 150 pounds or more. Because the turtle is more susceptible to large predators it is more aggressive on land. In the water, an adult alligator snapping turtle is docile because it is large and has almost no enemies except man.

Alligator Snapping Turtle

All turtles lay their eggs on land, in soil, sand, or decaying plant matter. The sea turtle waddles laboriously on flipperlike legs up from the waves onto the dry sand dunes far enough away from the high tides which might destroy the nest. Then, with her hind flipperlike legs, she digs a hole. Instinct tells her how to build her nest. She deposits the eggs and then covers them. The sea turtle builds her nest at such an angle that after most of the baby turtles have hatched it caves in, making it easy for the turtles to crawl out. Down within the dry warm sand, the eggs develop into baby turtles. The babies have a yolk sac attached to the center of their plastron. The yolk sac supplies them with food for a couple of days and the opening for the sac grows shut in a week or two. Maybe two hundred eggs hatch, but most of the turtles die within a week. Depending upon the species, there may be from one to three hundred eggs in a clutch, and some turtles lay two or three clutches a year.

Painted Turtle

The alligator snapping turtle has an unusual way of catching fish. Attached to its tongue is a wormlike appendage which it can wiggle back and forth to look like a worm and lure a fish. With open mouth the turtle waits for a fish to swim by. When one comes, the turtle wiggles the "worm" and the fish, thinking it has found food, swims near to eat the "worm" and at the same time the turtle with open mouth lunges for the fish. Then the jaws snap shut and the fish has disappeared.

Alligator Snapping Turtle

Box Turtle

Wood Turtle

The common snapping turtle can stretch its neck very far out, almost the length of its body. In the photograph, the tip of its nose is just sticking snorklelike out of the water so that it can breathe. The snapping turtle spends most of its time under water. Usually it is docile in the water but becomes aggressive and short tempered on land. Sometimes the yearlings of these snappers are found in pet stores, so if you handle one of them be careful not to put your hand close to its jaws because it can stretch its neck and give a severe bite.

These turtles grow a twenty-inch-long carapace and weigh as much as sixty pounds. The common snapping turtle is one of the most numerous fresh-water turtles and is found from the East Coast to the rocky mountains and from Canada to the Gulf of Mexico. In winter it hibernates under water. Sometimes several snappers will hibernate together in the mud but go their separate ways when they emerge in the spring. Many of these turtles are caught in traps, sent to markets, and sold as a delicacy in restaurants. The carapace of turtles which are sluggish is often coated with green algae. This makes an excellent camouflage for the turtle when it lies in wait for its prey. Then the powerful jaws can snap shut over an unwary fish.

Common Snapping Turtle

Diamondback Terrapin

Fresh-water turtles, like diamondbacks and painted turtles, swim with all four legs, using their webbed feet as paddles, pushing the water to the side. The legs move alternately, left front and right hind paddle together, then right front and left hind move together. As the turtle moves slowly through the water, it might make you think of a blimp or cruising submarine. Some turtles, like the red ear, have longer hind legs than front ones. When these turtles swim they use only their hind legs, kicking them alternately up and down while holding their front ones against their body. Soft-shelled turtles have webs between their toes and can swim fast.

Most turtles do not have lips. In fact, they do not even have teeth. Instead, their jaws are covered with a horny substance, have sharp edges, and are shaped like a beak. Turtles use this beak to bite off pieces of leaves, spears of grass, small fruits or, if they are eating an animal, to tear or rip it apart into bite-size chunks. They have a tongue which helps them swallow their food. You can see in the pictures how the diamondback pounces upon a shrimp, grabs with its beak, and pushes off part of the little animal with its claws.

Desert tortoises are herbivores or vegetable eaters. Box turtles are carnivorous when young, but eat plants as they grow older and seem to like mushrooms and fungi. Fresh-water turtles eat worms, snails, fish, polliwogs, crabs, toads, and plants. Turtles can smell food when they are under water. To do this they take a small amount of water in through their nose and let their Jacobson's organ sense the odors.

Diamondback Terrapin Eating Shrimp

Although a carapace of an ancient sea turtle has been found which measured twelve feet and probably, when the turtle was alive, weighed two tons, modern sea turtles may measure about four or five feet and weigh from 500 to 600 pounds. The Pacific ridley is one of the smallest sea turtles and when full grown weighs about eighty pounds. It has long front flippers which it flaps like bird's wings. Its hind legs are used as rudders to steer the turtle where it wants to go. The short legs are also used to make the turtle swim backward.

Ocean turtles eat and move at lower temperatures than land turtles. Sea turtles migrate to their breeding ground to mate and to lay eggs. They browse in fields or pastures of seaweed. As they grow older they also eat shrimp, crabs, fish, squids, and jellyfish.

Atlantic Ridley Turtle

Snakes

As you can see, in the drawing on the left, the skeleton of a snake consists of a skull, ribs, and a backbone with many vertebrae. Depending upon the species, it may have from 180 to 400 vertebrae. When a snake grows, it does not add more ribs to its body or more vertebrae to its tail. Instead its bones become larger as its body becomes bigger. Snakes in the United States grow to be from eight inches to eight or nine feet long.

The spine has five small joint surfaces in between each vertebrae which make it flexible. A network of muscles hooked onto each vertebrae controls the bending of the spine. A snake has two jaws which are hinged together. The lower jaw is made up of two pieces of bone which can move back and forth as well as to the sides. The ribs, which are not attached to a breastbone, can swing outward to make room for food to pass through the esophagus, stomach, small and large intestines, and cloaca. Also, like lizards, it does not have a large bladder. One lung is very small, while the other is almost as long as the body.

Herpetologists identify snakes by the number, shape, and size of scales around the head and by how many scales there are to a row on the back. Some scales are smooth; others have keels along the middle from base to tip. The scales on the back and at the sides are smaller than those on the undersides. Those on the belly are called plates or ventrals while those on the bottom of the tail are called caudals. The ventrals are oblong narrow and lie singly in a row across the underside.

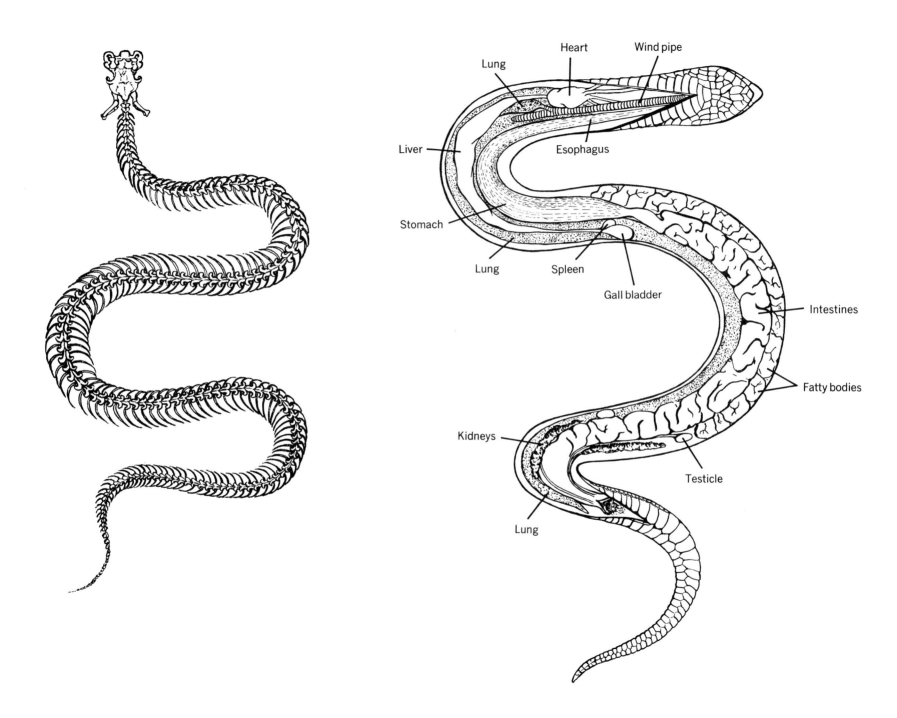

Lung

Heart

Wind pipe

Liver

Esophagus

Stomach

Lung

Spleen

Gall bladder

Intestines

Fatty bodies

Kidneys

Testicle

Lung

There are many kinds of snakes and often their names describe them. Some are named for their colors, such as green, scarlet, coral, or red-bellied, yellow-lipped. Often snakes are named after their physical features, such as short-tailed, sharp-tailed, flat-headed; and some, because of the patterns of scales on their heads, are named cone-nosed, hog-nosed, hook-nosed, or leaf-nosed.

Usually snakes which are kept as pets are docile and not inclined to be on the defensive as they might be if they were in the wild. People who have reptiles as pets believe that each animal has its own personality, just as there are behavior differences between puppies of the same litter.

For information about its surroundings, a snake depends upon its soft flexible Y-shaped tongue and its Jacobson's organ. In snakes this sense organ is made up of two saclike structures which are located toward the front of the roof of the mouth. Each sac has a short duct or tube. To sense its surroundings, the snake flicks out its tongue which picks up particles in the air or on the ground. Then the snake withdraws the tongue into the mouth and inserts the two tips into the two ducts. The Jacobson's organ then sends to the brain information such as, "A rat is near. It passed this spot just a moment ago."

Patch-nosed Snake

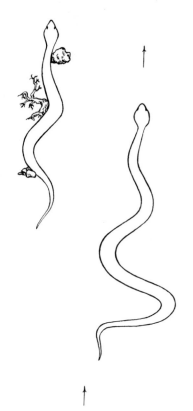

Snakes have several different ways of crawling. But all snakes can move by throwing their bodies into a series of waves of S curves. Strong muscles, which are attached to the sides of each vertebrae, contract and relax to bend the spine. Snakes can get enough traction to thrust their bodies forward by pushing each curve against a projection such as a pebble, clump of grass, exposed rock, or bump in the ground.

Long and thin snakes, like racers or whip snakes, throw their bodies into longer curves than short and fat snakes, like rattlesnakes, and consequently they are able to travel faster. This serpentine movement is used when snakes swim and when they climb bushes and trees.

Another way of crawling is by bunching up the S-shaped curves so that they lie close together like the bellows of an accordion and thrusting the head forward and then pulling up the body into another bunch of S curves. The weight and friction of the bunched curves give enough traction so that the snake can thrust its head forward.

Some snakes, like the sidewinder, instead of pushing the head forward, thrust it to the side. A few snakes, like rattlesnakes, can also use their belly or ventral scales to push-pull themselves along in a straight line. Because ventral scales protrude slightly and their free edges can swing forward and pull back, they are able to "grip" the ground like tractor treads. So that part of the body is off the ground and part of it is on the ground, the scales are divided into groups. Alternate groups of scales are raised, drawn forward, and then put down on the ground, while the rest of the body is pulled over them. Often snakes use different combinations of these movements, but whatever they do they travel quickly for an animal that has no legs. The fastest-moving snake, the coachwhip, probably cannot go more than four miles per hour which is about the speed at which a man walks.

Corn Snake

The longer snakes remain in the sunshine, the hotter their blood becomes. Rattlesnakes, if they are out too long in extremely hot sunshine, will die in about ten minutes. They cannot withstand temperatures over $100°$ F. Snakes have to keep their body temperature above $55°$ F. to move about. If their temperature goes much below $40°$ F. they become stiff and cannot move.

During the winter months snakes crawl into places where they will be protected from the extreme cold, and they will hibernate until the weather is warmer. Depending upon the climate, snakes hibernate from two to six months and will burrow down from three to thirty inches in the ground to be below the frost line.

Snakes often hibernate together and will crawl into protected places like crevices in cliffs, under rocks, stumps of trees. Often they will use abandoned burrows of rabbits, prairie dogs, muskrats, and rats. A burrow may contain anywhere from two to eighty snakes. Out in the prairies, where there are a lot of abandoned burrows close together as in a prairie dog town, there may be as many as seven hundred hibernating rattlesnakes. These congregating places are called den areas. Snakes which live in tropical climates go into estivation when it is too hot and dry or when it rains and is too wet.

The Sonora Whip Snake

Snakes have no eyelids and therefore cannot blink. Their eyes are protected by a transparent skinlike covering or eye scale. You might think of this eye scale as being like a contact lens except that it is attached to the skin of the snake and usually comes off when the snake molts. A few days before a snake molts, this eye scale turns an opaque milky white and the eyes look as though they had a film over them. At this time the snake is partially blind and often goes into hiding. Then two or three days before the actual molting begins, the eyes clear up. Sometimes the eye scale becomes stuck and does not come off with the shedding skin. If the snake is in a zoo, the keeper removes the eye scale with a pair of tweezers. However, if the snake is in the wild, the eye scale usually comes off with the following molt. If you look carefully at the eyes of the molting speckled king snake in the photograph, you will see that the old milky scales did not come off.

When a snake molts, the skin splits open at its nose and peals back like a glove, usually all in one piece. The snake secretes an oily solution under the old skin which lubricates and makes it easier for the snake to slip the old skin off. By rubbing and squirming, the snake will push the skin back over its head as well as under its chin and the whole skin rolls off toward the tail. The snake lifts and stretches each ventral scale on its underside as it slowly crawls out. It may take a snake several hours of wriggling or pushing against rocks or branches before the skin is completely off. The old skin looks like a piece of tissue-paper-thin plastic and feels soft and pliable. How often a snake molts depends upon how much it eats and how fast it grows. Usually a growing snake molts about every two months. The new skin is shiny, bright, and slightly moist, but it soon becomes dry. The colors are fresh and bright because the new scales are clear and have not yet become scratched and worn.

Common King Snake

Some snakes, like the corn, king, and gopher snakes, are constrictors. Constrictors kill their prey by constricting or squeezing their bodies around the animal so that it cannot breathe. When a constrictor catches and kills a mouse, it first lunges and grabs hold of the creature with its mouth. Then, almost at the same time, the snake wraps itself around the mouse. The snake does not squeeze so tightly that it purposefully crushes the ribs of the animal. When the mouse exhales and its chest contracts, the snake tightens its grip so that the mouse cannot expand and fill its lungs with air. Each time the mouse exhales a little more in an attempt to make room for more fresh air, the snake tightens its grip—until the mouse suffocates, its heart fails, and it dies in less than a minute. Then the snake turns the dead mouse around so that its head can be swallowed first.

It is easiest for a snake to start eating the head of the animal. For instance, if the snake is eating a bird and starts with the head, by the time the head and shoulders have entered the mouth and have gone into the throat, the wings fold against the body of the bird and easily slip into the mouth. If the snake had started to eat the feet first, the wings would stick out and would not go into the mouth. Sometimes, but not very often, a snake will stuff its mouth and throat with an animal too large for it to swallow. If the animal sticks in its throat and the snake is unable to regurgitate it, then the snake chokes, suffocates, and dies.

Gopher Snake

Because its teeth are pointed and curved backward like hooks, a snake does not use them to chew and has to eat its prey all in one piece. The jaws of a snake are able to open and stretch wide enough so that it can eat animals that are several times as wide as its body. Instead of being fused together, as is your lower jaw, the lower jaw of a snake is divided in the middle and has two movable bones, one on each side. These bones are connected at the front by an elastic ligament. These bones can move not only to the front, back, and out to the sides but up and down as well.

To swallow an animal the jaws go through a series of movements. For the first movement, one side of the lower jawbone moves forward, then, after the curved teeth have hooked into the flesh of the animal, this lower jawbone pulls back. For the second movement, the other side of the jawbone moves forward, hooks its teeth into the animal, and that jawbone pulls back. During the second movement, the first side releases its teeth and starts to move forward again. In this way each movement forces the animal farther down the throat. The snake continues this alternate pulling until the animal disappears into the throat where muscles contract and expand to push the food down into the stomach. On the opposite page you can see a snake eating a frog. As the snake grabbed the frog, its teeth punctured the flesh of the animal so that the saliva secreted by glands in the gums would enter the punctured holes and start the digestive process.

Common Garter Snake Eating Frog

Rattlesnake fangs–jaw
open in striking pose

Fangs folded back
against upper jaw

Often a rattlesnake, like the red diamondback in the photograph, lies coiled around itself, with its head pillowed on its own body. In this position it can quickly defend itself. Its head, neck, and upper body rise up to form an S, its striking pose. When a snake thrusts out its head to bite, we say it strikes. After a rattlesnake has bitten its prey, it waits a few minutes to let the poison in its digestive juices begin to work. The poison acts upon the nerves of the victim and slows down or stops body actions, especially those of the lungs and heart.

Each fang is a sharply pointed hollow tooth which acts like a hypodermic needle. The poison comes from a gland which is in the upper jaw and is connected to the tooth. The venom contains a very concentrated solution of digestive juices. So strong, in fact, that by the time the food has reached the stomach it is well digested. When a rattlesnake opens its mouth to use these fangs, they are swung up and outward, ready to stab the prey. The upper jaw has six hinged and movable bones which allow the snake to open its mouth very wide. Most snakes have two rows of teeth in their upper jaw but only one row in the lower. When a fang falls out, another grows in its place.

If you are ever around after a rattlesnake has been killed, stay away from its head. Its jaws may twitch open and shut, and could "bite" for several hours even though the animal is dead.

You cannot tell the age of a rattlesnake by the number of rattles on its tails. These horny rattles are part of its skin and one segment is formed each time the snake molts. Some rattlesnakes shed six times a year. However, the rattle often breaks off after six or eight segments have been formed, and a new series of segments then grow.

Red Diamondback Rattlesnake

Snakes have several ways of defending themselves. Some will rear their heads up as though they were going to strike, make a hissing sound, and inflate themselves to look bigger than they are. Some, like the rattlesnake, will stay perfectly still. Their protective patterns of color blend in with their surroundings so that you can scarcely see where they are. Often sidewinders and copperheads have been stepped upon because of their camouflage. Some, like the hog-nosed snake, will roll over and play dead. Other snakes when picked up will spray a smelly liquid. Some, like the rattlesnake, vibrate their tails as a warning. This behavior is mimicked by some snakes, like the gophers, and if their tail happens to rustle dry leaves, it can make a sound very much like a vibrating rattle.

After a snake has tried all of its ways to discourage the enemy, it will resort to biting. Snakes do not attack humans unless they are provoked or are so startled that they react automatically and strike. In fact, snakes are afraid of humans, and, unless they are cornered, will run away rather than stay and fight.

Pit vipers, such as rattlesnakes, copperheads, and water moccasins, are so called because they have a heat-sensing organ, or pit, at the side of their head. As you can see in the photograph, the pit, which is between its nostrils and eyes, looks like a deep dimple. The pit can sense temperature differences of as little as one degree within striking distance. This enables the snake to find its prey and accurately direct its strike—particularly at night.

Water Moccasin

Early in the spring the male and female snakes mate. When a female is pregnant we say she is gravid. Most gravid snakes stop eating when there is not enough room in their bodies for both food and eggs. Like lizards, snakes have a vent or opening to the cloaca at the base of their body. When a female lays eggs, they come out through this vent. In warm climates, most female snakes lay from thirty to one hundred eggs. Depending upon the species and the weather, the eggs hatch either within a few weeks or a couple of months.

The female snake deposits her eggs in holes under rocks and logs, or in abandoned burrows. Thus the eggs are somewhat hidden from predators and have a certain amount of protection from the heat during the day or from the cold at night. Sometimes eggs are laid under a blanket of leaves, in a haystack, leaf mold, decaying vegetation, or compost heap where they will be kept warm.

Snakes eggs, like lizard eggs, do not have a hard shell. Instead, they have a tough but leathery coating. Eggs vary in size from half an inch to two inches long and are usually oval in shape. Snake eggs are not as colorful as many bird eggs and are usually a drab cream or white color. In cold climates most snakes give live birth to their young. The chances for the young to survive are better with live births than with unprotected eggs. These snakes may have from one to eighty or more offspring in a brood.

Sidewinder

Most poisonous snakes have a triangular-shaped head, like the moccasin or rattlesnake. However, one poisonous snake, the coral, has a narrow head. There are two kinds of coral snakes in the United States. One is in the southern part of the Carolinas to Texas, and the other is in Arizona. Coral snakes look very much like the harmless scarlet snakes found from New Jersey to Florida and the harmless California mountain king. All of these snakes can be mistaken one for the other. Therefore, it is a good rule to leave all red-, black-, and white- (or yellow-) striped snakes strictly alone.

There is no need to kill a coral snake just because it is poisonous, and the same is true with other poisonous snakes. These snakes help keep the rodent population from becoming too large. All too often the harmless ones which look like rattlesnakes or coral snakes are killed and their death means there will be more rodents. So if you see what you think is a poisonous snake, just leave it alone.

California Mountain King Snake

HARRIET E. HUNTINGTON was born of New England parents in Florida and developed her love for books and writing in her father's large reference library. Her family moved to California when she was quite young. After her father died, she and her mother traveled extensively—several times to Europe and twice around the world.

After a brief stay at Briarcliff College and a nursery school training course at Broadoaks College (now Pacific Oaks College in Pasadena), she began her career as a children's book author with LET'S GO OUTDOORS and LET'S GO TO THE SEASHORE. These books were written in response to the many questions that children had asked her about nature and the outdoors.

She learned photography the hard way—by trial and error. But now, with more than a dozen books behind her, she has become a nationally known author and photographer.